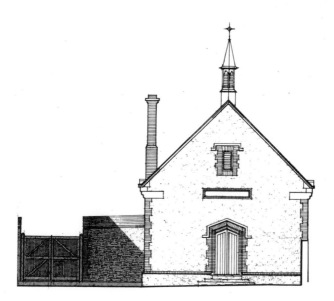

ISBN 0947338 56 X
Copyright © 1994 Axiom Publishers, Adelaide, South Australia
Cover art copyright © 1994 Migration Museum

Text by Mary-Louise Geyer
Design and layout by Sandra Rodda

Front cover: *Vida Catt, The archway into the Women's Quarters of the Destitute Asylum, 1920, oil on canvas, Migration Museum collection.*
Back cover: *The former Lying-in Home now the Migration Museum*
Title papers: *Architectural drawings for the restoration of the Lying-in Home (SACON Heritage Unit)*
Contents page: *Lamp outside the archway into the Women's Quarters of the Destitute Asylum (State Records, S.A.)*

BEHIND THE WALL

THE WOMEN OF THE DESTITUTE ASYLUM
ADELAIDE, 1852-1918

MARY GEYER

WOMEN'S SUFFRAGE CENTENARY
SOUTH AUSTRALIA 1894-1994

AXIOM PUBLISHERS
in association with the
MIGRATION MUSEUM
A division of the History Trust of South Australia

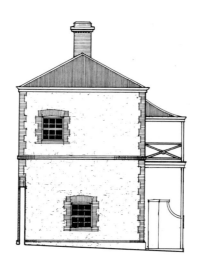

CONTENTS

FOREWORD

In 1986 the Migration Museum was opened in buildings which formerly had been the Women's Quarters of Adelaide's Destitute Asylum. The Migration Museum's brief is to present the history of immigration which has led to the development of the cultural diversity of South Australia.

Whilst researching the origins of the Destitute Asylum it was discovered that part of the site had been used for four years as a Female Immigration Depot. It was the pressure of thousands of women, all penniless, many pregnant and alone, which had prompted the colonial government to build special quarters which later included a Lying-in Home and Mothers' Wards. One of the permanent displays in the Museum is about the women and children who had lived behind the high stone wall on Kintore Avenue in the Destitute Asylum.

In 1994 with the assistance of a grant from the Women's Suffrage Centenary Committee it became possible to undertake further research to find out more about some of the women who had lived, worked, given birth, and died at the Destitute Asylum.

I would especially like to thank researcher and author Mary Geyer. Without her enthusiasm and additional hours of work this project could not have been completed. I would also like to thank all the descendants and relatives of Destitute Asylum inmates who responded to Mary's appeal for information. The social stigma of having been destitute, especially of having been an unmarried mother, unfortunately persists. We are therefore very grateful to those who came forward to share their family histories with us and to loan us documents and photographs.

I would also like to thank Christine Finnimore as editor, George Klein who introduced the Museum to Axiom Publishers and the Women's Suffrage Centenary Committee who funded the research.

Viv Szekeres,
DIRECTOR, MIGRATION MUSEUM.

BEHIND THE WALL

SHE WORE A SEVERE BLUE-GREY DRESS and a white apron like her fellow female inmates. The dress was standard issue and had been made by women who had lived behind the wall before her. It was not designed to flatter, but to last.

Her life was regulated by the Asylum bell. Because she was 'able-bodied' she spent her days washing and mending the bed linen and clothing of the other male and female inmates or assisting in the kitchen. Once a week she was permitted to leave the grounds for five or six hours. This privilege was tempered by the humiliation of the distinctive uniform. To be destitute was to be shamed.

This is the story of what she experienced as she endured life as one of South Australia's paupers. Who was she? Who were the countless other women who passed through the Destitute Asylum and Lying-in-Home before and after her? What became of them? What would they have done if there had not been a Destitute Asylum?

The bell from the Lying-in Home. It regulated the daily activities of the women who lived there. Migration Museum collection

The archway, built in 1854, which led into the
Women's Quarters in the Destitute Asylum
State Records (South Australia)

'IMPERFECT TIES OF A NEW SOCIETY'

Women in the Destitute Asylum, 1852-56

DEBORAH FITZGIBBONS WAS 24 YEARS OLD when she walked through the gothic arch leading into the single courtyard of the Destitute Asylum, on land now occupied by Artlab and the University of Adelaide, on a hot February day in 1856. The gatekeeper bolted the gate behind her while she stopped to look at the collection of buildings along the courtyard's southern and western boundaries and the stone wall around its northern and eastern perimeters. A number of women sat around in groups under the verandah of the women's quarters. Deborah smiled uncertainly under their blank gazes as she walked past them to the Comptroller's office with the note from her employer explaining that because of a chest ailment she was not able to work as a domestic servant. Deborah was destitute.

Deborah realised that many people had lives easier than hers, free from discomfort, worry and the judgements that were placed on her for what she was. Deborah undoubtedly wondered what she had done to deserve her many disadvantages. As a woman she was deemed physically and intellectually inferior to most men and her work was paid less than the equivalent work of male labourers. Deborah and other South Australian women were ineligible to vote, a right extended to most men in the South Australian Constitution Act which was passed later in June 1856. As a domestic servant and working woman, Deborah was considered inferior by the women who employed her. According to popular Victorian ideals a respectable woman's sphere was the home. She was expected to be maternal, meek, nurturing and pious and to fill her days with caring for her family. Her absence from the paid workforce was a testament to her husband's ability to support her. Obviously such a secure material existence was beyond Deborah's reach. Her work as a servant did not pay adequately for her to accumulate assets nor to buffer her from poverty. In times of illness or injury nothing and nobody stood between Deborah and destitution.

Deborah Fitzgibbons was alone and sick in South Australia. She was one of many colonists whose similar circumstances had led to the establishment of the Destitute Asylum on land between North Terrace and the River Torrens. (See Appendix 2.) The South Australian government had initially hoped that people such as she would be supported by family members. This hope had been enshrined in the 1843 Act of the South Australian Parliament to 'provide for the maintenance and relief of deserted wives and children and other destitute persons'. The Act stated that three generations of relatives were responsible for the maintenance of poor and destitute family members who were not able to work. Justices of the Peace were empowered to assess the means of relatives and, if possible, to order them to support needy kin. However, many colonists like Deborah had no relatives, either in South Australia or any of the other colonies. Although the Maintenance Act did not formally acknowledge the role of the government in the welfare of South Australia's colonists it implied that the government would support destitute people who did not have any relatives in the colony.

By 1856 the Destitute Asylum, providing 'indoor relief', was capable of housing 140 homeless and destitute persons. In March of that year it was home to 65 women, 30 men and 43 children. At this time the South Australian government provided rations through 'outdoor relief' to a further 693 people who lived in their own homes.

According to its regulations no 'able-bodied' person was allowed support in the Asylum. Only the sick such as Deborah, and the aged were admitted. Of the 65 women who resided in the Destitute Asylum's Women's Quarters in 1856 fifteen were either in the final stages of pregnancy or recovering from childbirth. Only a third were married. Of the other 50 female inmates of the Destitute Asylum, 30 were without relatives in the colony, including six widows. Thirty-three women were ill, injured or convalescent. Their ailments included rheumatism, chest infections, dysentery and sore eyes. Three women were suffering from venereal diseases. Two women were caring for their children. One woman had been deserted by her husband and two had husbands who were in the Destitute Asylum's Male Quarters. Three of the female inmates were Aboriginal women who had been sent to the Destitute Asylum from the Adelaide Gaol before being sent on to Port Lincoln. The Asylum staff classified the other nine women as imbeciles or lunatics. The average age of these 50 female inmates was 28 years.

Mrs Webber was one of the women who was caring for her children at the Destitute Asylum. We do not know her first name because the Asylum officer who admitted her did not list it. Upon marriage she had lost a considerable part of her individual identity to her husband. In March 1856 Mrs Webber and her two children had lived at the Destitute Asylum for seven weeks. Her husband was in Victoria, presumably at the goldfields. We do not know if he returned or if he felt any remorse about leaving his family to fend for themselves. However we do know that even after abandoning them to the mercy of the Destitute Board he still retained rights of custody of the children. Until the 1858 Matrimonial Causes Act he owned whatever money his wife may have earned, and indeed the very clothes she stood in, because as a married woman she did not have the legal right to own property. According to the law married women were protected by their husbands. In fact, many were exploited by them.

During the mid-1850s the South Australian government became increasingly alarmed by the prevalence of colonists such as Deborah Fitzgibbons and Mrs Webber. In 1856 a Select Committee of the Legislative Council enquired into 'the causes of the present large amount of destitution in the Colony, and the best means of diminishing the same'.

In his evidence before that Committee Matthew Moorhouse, Comptroller of the Destitute Asylum, described it as 'a sort of convalescent relief establishment for the Hospital ... every room in the place is now a hospital'. He stated that one-fifth of inmates were permanently ill or injured and that only two of the 138 inmates were able-bodied. When asked if he had 'any reason to hope that the present destitution might be so far decreased as to render the services of the Destitute Asylum Board no longer necessary', Moorhouse replied that:

there will always have to be a degree of relief afforded by the Government to some portion of the people. We have this morning (12 March 1856) the names of 125 widows on the books besides a number of orphans, and paralytic patients, and blind persons; and what are we to do with those poor people?

In his evidence Mr Tapley, the Relieving Officer, commented that recently-arrived colonists tended to receive relief temporarily while 'where relief is given to persons who have been longer in the Colony, it assumes a more permanent character, in consequence of their being aged and infirm persons'.

The Committee reported that the number of destitute persons relieved by the government had been growing steadily for a number of years. In 1853, the government relieved 464 persons. In the following year the number had risen to 685. In 1855 the colonial authorities gave assistance to a staggering 3,027 destitute.

The Committee suggested a number of reasons for the astonishing number of destitute persons during 1855: a bad harvest, which 'diminished employment and increased the cost of living'; an excess of female immigrants, 'which reduced the price of labor, and threw many out of work'; the failure of children to support their parents; the desertion of wives and children by men who left the colony to go to the Victorian goldfields; the incidence of men falling on hard times at the goldfields and, though willing, being unable to send funds to their families. There was also the numerous accidental deaths of miners who left widows and fatherless children in South Australia. The Committee felt that the 1843 Maintenance Act was not enforceable. They recognised the 'imperfect ties of a new society' and the government's responsibility to provide for destitute persons who did not have relatives who could support them. They were concerned, however, that the relief the government had provided was 'over-bounteous'. Their Report quoted Matthew Moorhouse who believed that the moment a public charity 'does more than meet the existing necessities of destitution, it begins the creation of a spirit of pauperism' . They recommended legislation to punish fraudulent applications for relief. The cost and discouragement of dependence on government relief were to continue to be primary concerns of colonial authorities throughout the history of the Destitute Asylum.

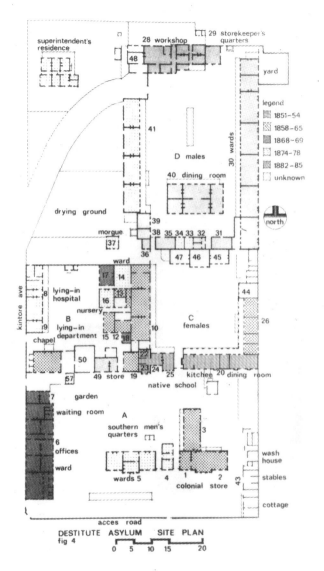

Plan of the site of the Destitute Asylum showing the development of the complex between 1851 and 1885 Courtesy SACON Heritage Unit

13

'EXCESSIVE FEMALE IMMIGRATION'

Female migrants, 1852-56

On a cool September day in 1855 Margaret Hanlon looked up from the trough she was bent over in the washing shed of the Adelaide Female Immigration Depot and gazed through the door . Her eyes flickered over the walled-in courtyard which had been her home for the last three weeks. A group of women were walking north across it with Mr Ennis, the Yard Overseer, who had selected them to meet prospective employers in Matron Ross' rooms. Margaret was not surprised that he had not chosen her. Who would want an unskilled domestic with crippled arms?

Margaret was among an excess of 5,112 single female immigrants who arrived in the colony between 1853 and 1855. They came contrary to the agreement between the South Australian Immigration Department and the Colonial Land and Emigration Commissioners in the United Kingdom which specified that equal numbers of men and women would immigrate to South Australia.

The excess of single female immigrants had become a burden on the colonial coffers by March 1855. At that time 96 recently-arrived single women were unable to gain employment as domestic servants and were supported by the South Australian government. By the end of June 1855 the number had risen to 470. During July, August and September an average of 772 women were maintained by the colonial authorities. However the Adelaide Female Immigration Depot, a quadrangle to the north of the Destitute Asylum, on land now part of the University of Adelaide, could accommodate only 60 women at a time. The rest were housed at the Destitute Asylum or in whatever makeshift accommodation could be found. Many women remained

*Workroom, drying and
washing rooms of the
Women's Quarters in
1918
State Records
(South Australia)*

*Women's boots from the
1890s which were found
under the floorboards of
the Lying-in Home during
its renovation for use as
the Migration Museum
Migration Museum
collection*

on the ships in which they had immigrated for up to two weeks after their arrival in South Australia.

The Adelaide Female Immigration Depot had to support the largest number of single female immigrants during the last three months of 1855. On 2 November the Depot supported 831 single women. By 20 December the number had dropped to 397.

The expense of supporting these women led the South Australian government to conduct an enquiry into 'Excessive Female Immigration' in 1856. The Select Committee of the Legislative Council not only found that the number of single female immigrants who arrived in South Australia between 1853 and 1855 had not been in proportion to the number of male immigrants who arrived in the colony during this time. Its investigations also revealed that, in conflict with the agreement between the South Australian and British immigration authorities, Irish women among these arrivals outnumbered immigrants from other areas of the United Kingdom. The Committee reported that the number of single female immigrants who arrived in South Australia between 1853 and 1855 exceeded the demand for female workers in the colony by an amount that Matthew Moorhouse, Superintendent of the Adelaide Female Immigration Depot, estimated at 100 per month.

At this time most of South Australia's paid female workforce was employed in domestic service. However, the Select Committee found that most of the single females who immigrated to South Australia between 1853 and 1855 were not experienced as domestic servants, nor did they have the ability to adapt themselves readily to other fields of employment.

The Select Committee roundly criticised the Colonial Land and Emigration Commissioners in the United Kingdom for sending such a vast number of unskilled, unprotected and potentially dependent females to the colony. The Select Committee drew attention to the fact that many of the single female immigrants who had arrived in Adelaide had originally obtained disembarkation orders for Melbourne or Sydney. These women worried the Committee for two reasons: not only were they shipped to Adelaide at the expense of the South Australian Immigration Fund, but the colony was having to support them until they could arrange transport to their intended destinations. South Australia therefore was carrying the costs of supplying labour to other Australian colonies.

In the course of its investigation the Select Committee examined 26 women who had lived at the Adelaide Female Immigration Depot after their arrival in South Australia between 1853 and 1855.

Margaret Hanlon was among the witnesses questioned by the Committee. She was a widow in her late 30s who had arrived in South Australia with her 21 year-old daughter aboard the *Admiral Boxer* in August, 1855. Margaret came from Naas, in County Kildare, where she had 'kept house' for her father. She came to South Australia because she was in economic difficulties. Her sister, who was employed in Adelaide as a domestic servant, sent her money and paid part of her fare. At the enquiry Margaret showed the Committee her 'two crippled hands and forearms frightfully wasted', explaining that they were the legacy of an attack of small-pox. The Committee questioned Margaret about medical examinations prior to emigrating because she should not have passed the fitness test. She explained that she was capable of washing and similar tasks, remarking that 'it is wonderful how much I can do, considering the extent of my affliction'. Margaret testified that she had lived at the Adelaide Female Immigration Depot for five weeks before her brother-in-law found her a job as a nursemaid. Margaret told the Committee that she continued to receive relief from the Depot because her wages were so small. She stated that after she paid half of her weekly wage of 12 shillings in rent she was not left with enough money to support herself.

The Select Committee of the Legislative Council also reported on the number of single immigrant women who gave up their placements of work and returned to the support of the Depot. There were various opinions on this matter. In her evidence Matron Ross stated that most women were returned to the depot by their employers 'on the plea that they are useless'. Matthew Moorhouse, in his role as the Superintendent of the Adelaide Female Immigration Depot, and other witnesses stated that the women were unskilled and best suited to tasks such as milking and 'rough farm work'. A more sympathetic witness was Mr Ennis, Yard Overseer. He told the Committee that many young girls had 'been frightened by the state in which girls' hands were on returning from service in the country'. In response to the sceptical questioning of the Committee Mr Ennis explained that many of the women who returned from country service were experienced domestics. They returned 'knocked about ... overworked', with 'their hands stripped'. He described the work of one woman, who had 'twenty cows to milk, to churn without assistance, and a great deal of work besides'. His testimony was supported by the evidence of a number of female immigrants who explained that their health had been broken by the work they were expected to do in both country and town placements. They had returned to the Depot to recover.

The women and girls worked within the Depot. Some sewed hessian sacks for the firm of Dutton and Macdermott in exchange for boots for themselves. Others, using cotton supplied by a 'Committee of Ladies', made garments, stockings and embroidered items which they sold. They were allowed to keep their earnings. A group of women who were lacemakers left the Depot and set up a lacemaking establishment in a rented room.

The women also tried as best they could to be cheerful in their drab surrounds. When asked by the 1856 Inquiry if there was 'any recreation at the Depot, any music or dancing?' Mr Ennis, the Yard Overseer, replied that 'the girls sing sometimes' but that he knew 'nothing of any musical instruments' being played.

The Committee reported finally that in over 60 per cent of cases women returned to the Immigration Depot 'with testimonials of honest, industrious and exemplary conduct'. However in order to cut expenses the Committee advised that the terms of readmission be made stringent and that returned servants should contribute to the cost of their maintenance. In their recommendations to keep down the cost of maintaining those in need and to discourage dependence on the government the Committee reiterated their earlier concerns.

In its Report the Committee noted that single female immigrants had stopped arriving in the colony and expressed the hope that 'the day is not remote when the remaining burden ... shall cease to be oppressive'. The crisis of providing for the excess numbers of single female immigrants did pass in the next few months and the Adelaide Female Immigration Depot closed before the end of 1856. Its buildings were used as a military hospital and then became part of the Destitute Asylum's Male Quarters in 1870.

One of the buildings used for the Female Immigration
Depot in the 1850s being demolished in 1918
State Records (South Australia)

'THE PROPER OBJECTS OF RELIEF'

Women in the Asylum, 1860s and 1870s

BY THE 1870S THE ASYLUM had grown considerably from the structure Deborah Fitzgibbons knew in 1856. The original quadrangle where she had lived and which had accommodated 140 homeless destitute people was now exclusively used for female inmates. Men who were admitted to the Asylum were housed in a group of buildings to the south around the Armoury and Barracks buildings that remain today. Men and women were strictly segregated, separated by a thick stone wall approximately nine feet (2.8 metres) tall.

Despite the increasing demand for food and accommodation for the destitute in South Australia during the 1850s and early 1860s, the colonial authorities were reluctant to establish a workhouse in the colony on the English model. Such an institution was in conflict with the principles behind the 1836 foundation of South Australia. According to the Wakefieldian theory of 'Systematic Colonisation', the emigration of the correct proportions of capital and labour from Britain to the new province would create an ideal society free from the social, political and economic problems which plagued industrial Britain. It was believed that the new settlement would be self-sustaining, prosperous and virtuous. There would not be any need to provide for paupers because poverty would not exist. Temporary difficulties caused to some workers and their families by uncertain seasons could be alleviated by aid given to them in their own homes.

Reluctantly, however, South Australian legislators came to realise that there were homeless and helpless poor whose needs could not be met by small, temporary subsidies to their income. Their answer, expressed in legislation and erected as stone and brick as the Destitute

Asylum, was a separate institution where the poorest and most dependent could be regulated and hidden from the affronted gaze of respectable citizens.

In 1863 the South Australian government passed its second piece of legislation dealing with social welfare. Although the 'Act for the regulation of the Asylum for the Destitute Poor' did not define the 'deserving poor' or validate the Destitute Board's existence, it empowered the Governor to make rules for the management of the Asylum. It imposed penalties upon inmates who broke the Asylum's regulations, or obtained relief under false pretences or stole Asylum property. It also empowered justices or magistrates to order the repayment of the cost of maintenance within three years should the recipients, or their relatives, be able to do so. The Act reflected the government's alarm at the growing number of people requiring relief and its attempts to keep their numbers to an absolute minimum. Despite these measures 1,276 colonists, or one in 125, were on government relief during 1865. Approximately 150 of these lived in the Destitute Asylum.

In 1867 a journalist from the *Register* visited the Asylum and gave a highly critical account of the standard of accommodation. He thought that the buildings were unsuitable, unplanned and inconvenient. 'There is hardly a good room in the whole establishment. The dormitories are small, and for the most part low and ill-ventilated'. He found an acute shortage of space and thought the Asylum was not as 'clean and comfortable as a Government establishment should be' even though care was 'evidently taken to keep the women's apartments clean and wholesome'.

That same year the Destitute Persons Relief Act formally established the Destitute Board and its functions and duties. The Board was empowered to appoint staff, administer funds voted by Parliament, manage the institutions under its control and 'have the ordering of the persons and property' belonging to the destitute while they remained under the Board's care. Under the terms of the Act, which re-emphasised the legal responsibility of relatives to provide for needy family members, the Destitute Board was able to inquire into and decide upon 'the proper objects of relief'. The Act included a clause which permitted a married woman whose husband had deserted her, or

View of the quadrangle and women's ward.
The photograph was taken in 1918 after the closure
of the Asylum.
State Records (South Australia)

The rear, south-facing, wall of the Women's Quarters. The photo was taken in 1924 after the closure of the Destitute Asylum.
State Records (South Australia)

Rear wall and archway of the Women's Quarters
State Records (South Australia)

been jailed, or declared an idiot or a lunatic to receive relief 'in the same manner and subject to the same conditions as if she was a widow' because at this time married women did not have the legal right to own property.

Ann Young was not a widow nor a deserted wife but her husband could no longer look after her. Her life had been harsh. She had worked hard as a domestic servant for the 32 years she had lived in South Australia. How sharp was the contrast between the dreams she had held of life in the new province when she stepped ashore in 1838 and her present circumstances! She had expected a secure old age, protected by her children, but God had not seen fit to bless her with any. Instead she had been cursed with a paralysis which had gradually crept upon her and deprived her of the ability to earn a living. She was even denied the dignity of ending her days in her own home in Walkerville. Her husband William had done what he could for her during the five years that she had been unable to move, but now aged 70 he was no longer able to cope. So it was that on 16 January 1871 Mrs Young, aged 62 years, became 'a proper object of relief' and was admitted to the Destitute Asylum.

Her existence in the Women's Quarters was controlled by 24 Asylum regulations that were established as a result of the 1866-7 Act. She heard the Asylum bell ring five times a day: at 7 am for able-bodied inmates to get out of bed; at 8 am for breakfast; at 12 noon or 1 pm on Sundays for lunch; for the evening meal at 5 pm; and at 8.45 pm, 'the lights being extinguished at 9 precisely'. Ann Young did not leave her bed all day because she was paralysed.

The Destitute Board Regulations stated that Asylum inmates had to clean themselves daily and bathe at least once a week. Ann needed help with these tasks. She relied on others to make her bed and sweep her ward daily. Once a week they cleaned her bedstead and aired her bedding. She knew that the other women worked in the Asylum's laundry, helped in its kitchen and made clothes for the inmates.

Ann's paralysis meant that she missed out on one of the few privileges extended to Asylum inmates, that of leaving the premises. The regulations permitted healthy female inmates to go out on Mondays at 11 am. They were required to return to the Asylum by 4 pm during the winter months of May to September. For the rest of the year they were permitted to stay out until 5 pm. However, Ann could see visitors (except persons 'of notoriously bad character') between 2 pm and 5 pm on Wednesdays. Ann felt sorry for her ward mates who were separated from their children. They were only allowed to see them for two hours between 12 and 2 p.m. on the last Monday of each month.

Mrs Young was typical of the aged and incurable for whom the Asylum was a last refuge. An article in the *Register* newspaper of 9 September 1872 quoted Thomas Reed, Chairman of the Destitute Board, who commented that 'as the Colony grows older it is found that whilst temporary relief may increase or lessen from causes more or less exceptional, permanent relief will probably increase'. In 1872, 2,085 colonists received outdoor relief from the Destitute Board, while 176 males, 56 females and 15 pregnant women resided at the Destitute Asylum. The paper reported that of these 247 inmates '75 per cent will most likely never quit it except by death'.

Ann Young died at the Destitute Asylum on 8 December 1874 at the age of 65 years. She had lived behind its walls for nearly four years. She was probably one of many Asylum inmates who were buried at the government's expense in simple coffins and unmarked graves in common ground at the West Terrace Cemetery.

Elizabeth Watson (1819-1908).
Elizabeth was born in Kent. She eloped and
immigrated to South Australia in 1839. She and her
husband William settled at Terowie where they had
twelve children. Most of the children died before
1890. After William's death in 1896 Elizabeth lived
with a daughter. She lent one of her sons a
substantial amount of money which he failed to
repay. Because her son-in-law did not wish to
accommodate her any longer Elizabeth was admitted
to the Women's Quarters of the Destitute Asylum in
October 1899.

Happily for Elizabeth her grandson came to her aid
after she had been in the Asylum for nine months.
She died at Terowie at the age of 90.

'A HOSPITAL FOR THE AGED, DECREPIT OR DISEASED'

Women in the Asylum, 1880s to 1917

CHRISTINA PEARSON SAT ON THE SIMPLE WOODEN BENCH in the waiting room of the Destitute Asylum for the first time on a December day in 1881. She was 39 years old. The Adelaide Hospital had written to the Destitute Board asking it to admit her to the Asylum while her feet healed. She had lost contact with her family and had nowhere to stay. Perhaps she was thinking about her husband and her children while she waited to see the Asylum's Superintendent.

Christina was born in Inverness in Scotland in 1842. She emigrated to South Australia aboard the *David Malcolm* in 1855 and married Robert Pearson in Kanmantoo, South Australia, in 1858. The couple had at least five children. Christina left her husband in 1878 'in consequence of him having taxed her with infidelity, of which she was not guilty'. She moved from Naracoorte to Adelaide and took up work as a domestic servant. She apparently never saw her husband or her children again.

Christina was admitted to the Destitute Asylum as a 'convalescent from hospital suffering from bad feet'. The Asylum's Superintendent recorded her particulars in the Register of Admissions. She used an alias probably because she was ashamed of her circumstances. She followed the Matron who showed her to the room in the Women's Quarters that she was to share with other female inmates. The Matron instructed Christina to wash and change into the Asylum's blue-grey uniform and told her where and when to get her meals.

The food that Christina and her companions ate during the week was detailed in the 1885 Report on the Destitute Act. For breakfast and the evening meal they ate dry bread and drank tea. Their lunch consisted of vegetable soup, boiled mutton or beef and potatoes. There were vegetables other than potatoes twice a week. One person's daily allowance was: 453g of bread, 226g of beef or 340g of mutton, 14g of tea, 57g of rice, 57g of sugar and 7g of salt. This dreary diet was only improved after Catherine Helen Spence, the social reformer, became a member of the Destitute Board in 1897.

For her time Christina was not a typical inmate of the Destitute Asylum. By the middle of the 1880s men outnumbered women in the Asylum by more than three to one. Christina was in her 30s when the average age of the female inmates was 64 years. Christina expected her feet to heal and then to be able to earn her living once more. Very few of the women inmates were able-bodied. Of the 115 women in the Asylum in June 1885, 50 were confined to their beds and approximately the same number were only just able to walk about. Five women were blind and a few were classified as 'imbecile' and 'lunatic'.

The 1885 Report of a Royal Commission into the Destitute Act of 1881 states that 'Practically the only occupation for the inmates capable of any kind of work is such employment as may be found for them in the ordinary routine of the Asylum'. The Commissioners reported that only 59 of the Asylum's 385 male and female inmates had 'any duties, however light'. It described the Destitute Asylum as 'a hospital for the aged, decrepit, or diseased' rather than a workhouse such as those in Britain.

The Destitute Board's annual reports contradicted the findings of the Commission regarding the 'light' duties given to the women. Those capable of work were employed in the traditional women's trades of laundry work and sewing garments and furnishings. The laundry work alone, which included the washing from the Royal Adelaide Hospital, earned the Asylum Board nearly half the costs of running the Lying-in Department. The work was so strenuous that the women who worked in the laundry went on strike in 1888. When he reported the strike to the Board in August of that year the Chairman recommended the sacking of a staff member who had supported the inmates in the strike. The Annual Report for 1887 details the number of items sewn in the Asylum during the previous year. The women had made a total of 2,729 articles such as dresses, flannel shirts and aprons, as well as ration bags, sheets, towels and window blinds. The Destitute Board thus employed the female inmates in partial competition with those women outside the Asylum who earned their living by washing and sewing, and in that way contributed to the causes of female destitution.

The Royal Commission identified deserting husbands as the chief cause of female pauperism. Twelve of the women who lived in the Destitute Asylum at the time of the Commission's Report had husbands who were deserters, and the Commission reported that nearly one-seventh of outdoor relief cases were the wives and children of men who had similarly absconded. The Report recorded the testimony of Thomas Reed, Chairman of the Destitute Board, who described desertion as 'the greatest abuse in our present system'. Reed suggested that fines or imprisonment were not sufficient punishments for men who left their dependants to fend for themselves. 'In vexation of soul' he recommended flogging them. The Commissioners' objection to such a penalty was that it would make it even more difficult to catch deserters. They placed their hopes upon intercolonial legislation to deal with the problem. But such laws did not eventuate until after Federation.

The Commission attributed 'the increase of outdoor relief' to 'commercial depression'. However it voiced contemporary attitudes when it believed poverty to be symptomatic of moral failing. The Commission believed that social problems led to poverty and that 'intemperance, improvidence, idleness and vice' were 'fruitful sources, here and everywhere, of pauperism'. The Commissioners believed further that the government was actively encouraging social dependence by the availability of its support.

The Commission considered the fifty-year-old model of the 1834 Poor Law of the United Kingdom, which strictly speaking did not provide 'outdoor' rations to those in need. The 1834 Poor Law's only provision for relieving poverty was indoor relief in the notorious workhouses of urban and rural England though in practice outdoor relief continued as before. The 'idle' poor, it was popularly thought, would find the alternative of the workhouse to an honest day's work so degrading and miserable that they would be forced back into the labour market, thus ensuring that the community would only have to support 'deserving' cases of poverty. The South Australian Royal Commissioners acknowledged that the provision of only 'indoor relief or the withdrawal of any relief' would reduce the costs of supporting the poor in the colony. However the Commission advised against the adoption of the British system because the cost of maintaining the needy at the Destitute Asylum was nearly three times the expense of outdoor relief. Apart from the cost the Commissioners had important social reasons for favouring the retention of outdoor relief. They believed that outdoor relief enabled 'widows and deserted wives, and women whose husbands are disabled from work, to bring up their families respectably, instead of seeking refuge in the Asylum, and it often helps the deserving poor to tide over a temporary emergency without breaking up their homes'.

The Royal Commission devoted some of its attention to the recurring theme of checks on immigration as a means of keeping down the cost of poor relief. The Commissioners observed:

> *Our statute book has prohibited the landing of convicts on our shores; it requires ships and passengers from ports infected with dangerous diseases to be quarantined ... but it contains no provisions for securing that imbecile or infirm persons, who may be shipped from other places to South Australia, shall not, immediately upon their arrival, become chargeable to the public.*

As an alternative the Commissioners suggested that South Australia follow the example of Victoria. By Victorian law a master of a ship that brought a 'lunatic, idiotic, deaf, dumb, blind or infirm' passenger into the colony was responsible for that passenger's maintenance for five years.

The inmates of the Asylum became recipients of public charity in other forms. A popular attraction for any South Australian in 1887 was a visit to the Jubilee Exhibition on North Terrace. The Exhibition Secretary wrote to the Destitute Board to say that Asylum inmates could visit the displays 'provided they are sent in batches' of not more than 25, 'under proper supervision and not on Wednesdays or Saturdays'.

Male and female inmates were segregated for such visits. The rules regarding segregation were so strictly enforced that when, in 1887, the staff discovered that men and women inmates conversed through ventilation ducts in the Women's Quarters, they requested that the ducts be altered. There were other entertainments. In 1889 a group of young people, who called themselves the Willing Workers, visited the Asylum and 'regaled the inmates' with 'a sumptuous treat'. In that same year the City of Adelaide Treasurer and the *Register* office donated five and three guineas respectively to be spent on 'Christmas Cheer' for the inmates.

When all else failed many South Australians still found a roof, bed and meals at the Asylum. In the late 1880s and early 1890s South Australia suffered drought, rural crisis and high unemployment. Economic crisis and greater demands for recognition from workers and from women led to new directions in social legislation. In 1883 married women were allowed to own property and assets in their own names. In some instances they could retain custody of their children. (See Appendix 2.) In 1894 women gained the right to vote in the elections for the colonial Parliament. In 1896 women who had been forced to leave violent and abusive husbands had a right to the government maintenance allowed widows and deserted wives. Parliament also debated the possible introduction of a pension for the aged as an alternative to support by the Destitute Board. This measure was passed by the Australian Federal government in 1909. Two years later a South Australian Labor government introduced a widows pension and empowered the Destitute Board to make cash payments to ill or injured persons. The legislation of 1909 and 1911 substantially reduced demands on the Destitute Asylum. It closed in 1917 when the Old Folks Home opened at Magill.

'FALLEN' *Women in the Lying-in Home, 1852-56*

WE DO NOT KNOW IF ANN KEENAN hung her head in shame or if she set her jaw against the judgement of colonial South Australia with a defiant glint in her eye, but we can be sure that she had never been as frightened in all her life as when she arrived in January 1856 at the Destitute Asylum's Lying-in Department.

Ann Keenan was a 19-year-old, unmarried, pregnant woman facing the most dangerous and painful time in her life without a single relative in South Australia. She was one of fifteen women either in the final stages of pregnancy or recovering after childbirth who lived in the original courtyard of the Destitute Asylum in March 1856. At the time there was only accommodation for nine lying-in women. The remaining six women were probably sheltered in the general Women's Quarters. The average age of these fifteen women was 24 years. Five of the fifteen were married. Their husbands were in the bush, on the goldfields, unemployed or in the Asylum's Male Quarters. The remaining ten women, including three widows, had no relatives in South Australia.

Despite the severity of their plight women such as Ann Keenan were seldom offered sympathy or treated with compassion by their fellow colonists. The moral code of Victorian society damned these women rather than alleviated their distress. By engaging in sexual relations outside of marriage Ann, and the countless other unmarried mothers who gave birth in the Destitute Asylum's Lying-in Home, had broken an important social restraint that was placed upon women. Motherhood was the ideal social and biological role for women, as symbolised by Queen Victoria and her children. But it was not acceptable for women, either married or unmarried, to behave as sexual beings. This fundamental aspect of women's individual human identity was regarded as a threat by the male guardians who 'protected' and controlled them. According to the social values of the day women were expected to be maternal, pure, domestic angels, removed from the desires of the flesh. The subjugation of women by men also had an economic dimension. Men were traditionally 'breadwinners' and their wages reflected this role. Women's employment was poorly paid, keeping them financially dependent on male guardians. Apart from being regarded as 'fallen' a woman such as Ann Keenan represented a threat to the values of colonial society.

In the first years of the Destitute Board's existence there was some controversy about whether single, destitute, pregnant women such as Ann Keenan should be considered South Australia's 'deserving poor'. Many people believed that the 'immorality' of these women cancelled out their claim to assistance. Since no other government institution would take them in the Board accepted responsibility for destitute pregnant women during their confinement.

The Board did, however, try to recover the costs of maintaining the pregnant women whenever possible. Under the 1843 Maintenance Act of the South Australian Parliament both mothers and fathers of illegitimate children were responsible for supporting them 'provided that no man shall be taken to be the father of any illegitimate child upon the oath of the mother only'. This meant that if the putative or alleged father denied paternity the mother had to present proof of a liaison with him, in the form of letters in which he acknowledged paternity, or a witness who could testify to an acknowledgement. While the maternity of the women who were admitted to the Lying-in Home could not be denied, the paternity of putative fathers often was. In the majority of cases putative fathers simply denied a connection with the pregnant woman, claimed she was a prostitute, or vanished. In evidence given to the 1856 Select Committee on Destitution Matthew Moorhouse, Comptroller of the Destitute Asylum, cited the example of a man 'who was the reputed father of three illegitimate children. The mothers of those children were two young girls and a widow ... He admitted having intercourse with the girls, but denied that he was the father, and alleged the girls were common prostitutes. Being threatened with legal proceedings he went off to Melbourne'. Though Moorhouse believed the statements of the girls who claimed that the man really was the father of their children, the Destitute Board was powerless to take any further action on the matter. Moorhouse stated that 'a considerable portion of the expense of carrying on the Destitute Asylum is incurred in consequence of the number of illegitimate children there, and ... in consequence of not being able to fix the paternity of the child'.

The Select Committees of 1856 identified two groups of 'undeserving' unmarried pregnant women: prostitutes and 'immoral' single female immigrants. The Relieving Officer of the Destitute Asylum, Robert Tapley, told the Select Committee on Destitution that pregnant or diseased prostitutes would come to the Asylum and 'throw themselves down at the door' and would 'not go away'. He said that after they got better they would not work and became 'impudent'. He also reported that the same women would return again and again. In some cases, diseased women returned four or five times to the Asylum to be cured, and some pregnant women had been confined three times at the Asylum. When a Committee member asked Tapley if there should be a rule that the Asylum would not admit a second pregnancy, Tapley explained that it was already a rule but that necessity demanded it be broken. He gave an example where 'a female comes to the Asylum pregnant or diseased, and is refused admittance. She goes up to the Police Court, and comes back to the Asylum accompanied by a policeman with a request from (the Presiding Magistrate) that she should be taken in, she is taken in'.

The 1856 Select Committee on Excessive Female Immigration asked its witnesses numerous questions about the prevalence of single female immigrants 'expecting to be confined soon after landing in the Colony' or suffering from venereal diseases. In his evidence Dr Duncan, head of the South Australian Immigration Department, stated that there were 'occasional cases of pregnancy among the single women who arrive, but they are not very frequent'. On the other hand Robert Tapley reported that nine women had been sent from the Adelaide Female Immigration Depot to the Lying-in room at the Destitute Asylum during January and that an average of three per month had been sent during the previous year. However most of these women had been in the colony for some time. Tapley stated that it was 'evident there has been some misconduct, for the Depot Board have prepared a room in the Destitute Asylum especially for the treatment of cases of venereal disease'. He thought that these women were not among those who had returned to the Depot after a period of employment. He believed they were women 'who had not been out of the Depot, except daily, to go through the town'. He expressed the opinion that many of these women had become 'immoral' on the voyage to South Australia because they were not sufficiently 'protected'. He recounted that he knew 'from good authority that the girls get over the wall into the Depot when they have been out beyond the time, and have been assisted to climb over by the soldiers they have been in company with'. He stated that 'there are almost always some men lurking about near the Depot. It is more quiet than it used to be about there, but the evil is not entirely suppressed'.

William Gosse, the Acting Colonial Surgeon, denied that any women had been removed from the Depot to the Asylum because they were suffering from venereal diseases. He believed that most of the women who went from the Depot to be confined at the Destitute Asylum were pregnant when they left Britain.

The 1856 Select Committees offered no recommendations on prostitutes or single female immigrants who sought shelter at the lying-in room of the Destitute Asylum. Perhaps their members realised that neither legislation nor moral condemnation could deny the desperate women who came to the Destitute Asylum as their sole refuge.

'IF HER CHILD SHALL SO LONG LIVE'

Lying-in women, 1860s to 1880s

JANE ROBERTS LAY IN THE NARROW BED and stared at what she could see of the mild autumn day out the window of the grim little lying-in room on the eastern boundary of the original quadrangle of the Destitute Asylum. Jane had not slept well. She tried not to think about the screams in the night, the flickering lights, the anxious midwife and the doctor shouting instructions. She tried to think of pleasant things. It was Wednesday. Perhaps her friend Sarah would visit her? It was not likely that she would have made the trip to town from Yorke Peninsula, but Jane clung to the hope just the same.

Jane shifted in the bed in a vain attempt to get comfortable. Her thoughts turned yet again to Charles Larson. She had long given up all hope that he would honour his promise to support his child. Jane cursed him bitterly as she thought of him under the sky she could just glimpse, cheerfully going about his business as the second mate of the *Bosphorus* many miles away. She wondered dully if he ever thought of her as she reluctantly contemplated her swollen body. The coming child had stolen her pride, her ability to earn a living, and, indeed, was going to be an economic and social burden. She knew it was wicked but she hoped that it would not live since that would be her only escape from the injustice of her fate.

Jane Roberts had good cause to fear for her own life. Although she would be attended by an experienced midwife during the birth of her child a doctor would not be summoned unless it was a complicated birth. By the time he arrived it could be too late for both mother and baby. In 1871 when Jane Roberts gave birth in the Lying-in ward of the Destitute Asylum many practising doctors had qualified without a

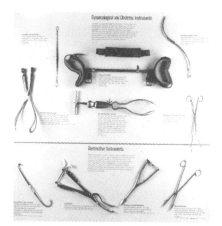

Midwives and doctors who attended the women who were confined in the Lying-in Home used gynaecological and obstetric instruments like these.
Collections of the Queen Victoria Hospital and Migration Museum

This view, taken in 1918, shows the Reformatory Girls' Day School on the left. The rear of the building had two rooms which were the labour and birthing wards of the Lying-in Home. The building still stands today and houses the Migration Museum's Forum Gallery and other exhibition areas.
State Records
(South Australia)

sound knowledge of obstetrics. Even if a mother and her baby survived the birth there was no guarantee that they would live for much time beyond it. Their recovery was never certain. 'Debility' or infection of the uterus after birth and the death of infants through bacteria and neglect were not uncommon in the overcrowded, poorly ventilated conditions of the Destitute Asylum.

There were many women who, like Jane Roberts, hoped that their children would not live. Although outside the law and punishable as crimes, abortion and infanticide were the inevitable results of the lack of reliable methods of contraception. The cost of raising a child, loss of earning capacity during pregnancy and the social stigma of bearing an illegitimate child drove an unknown number of women to illegal abortionists or to murder their new-born children.

Many women who terminated their pregnancies paid with their lives. Haemorrhaging and blood poisoning were common causes of their death. A small number of South Australian women were prosecuted with 'concealment of birth' or murder of their child through suffocation or neglect. The women were convicted and sentenced to hang but had their sentences commuted to imprisonment with hard labour. In 1870 Mary Partington, a 36 year-old widowed mother of six, was sentenced to hang for killing her new-born infant but the sentence was altered to fourteen years hard labour. Her six children, aged between three and fourteen years, were committed to the Destitute Asylum.

A greater demand for accommodation for destitute pregnant women than was available in the Lying-in ward meant that many of them were confined in the Asylum's general Women's Quarters. In 1867 the Destitute Board complained that it was not possible to separate pregnant women from other female inmates. They were concerned for two reasons: they believed that 'fallen' women were a bad influence upon the other girls and women in the Asylum, and it was distressing for these inmates to hear them in labour, particularly in complicated births. In the late 1870s increasing pressure for the accommodation of pregnant destitute women forced the South Australian government to finance a separate building for them.

On 21 August 1876 a letter to the *Register* signed 'Humanitarian' drew the attention of South Australians to the case of Ellen Wilson.

Annie Schar (1857-1935).
Born Anne Jephson she immigrated to South
Australia from Ireland in 1877. She married Peter
Carlsen, a seaman, at Port Adelaide in the following
year and in 1879 had a daughter by him. Peter was
reported lost at sea and Annie went to live at Venus
Bay where she worked as a domestic servant. In
1884 she became pregnant and while she was able to
identify the father of the child she had no proof of
paternity. She was admitted into the Lying-in Home
and her four year-old daughter was sent to the
Industrial School at Magill. Annie's second child
was stillborn. She returned to the West Coast with
her daughter and there married for a second time.

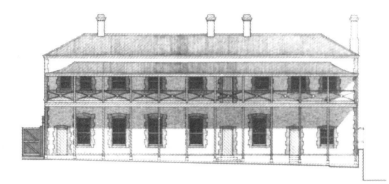

Eastern elevation of the Lying-in Home and Destitute Asylum chapel from plans drawn for the restoration of the building in the 1980s
Courtesy SACON Heritage Unit

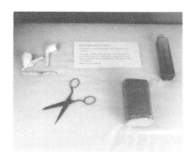

Relics from the Destitute Asylum which were recovered during restoration work on the site
Migration Museum collection

Bench from the Destitute Asylum Chapel
Migration Museum collection

Mrs Wilson had died in her home after a complicated birth that was not attended by a doctor. When medical help had been sought for Mrs Wilson it had been refused. The baby survived and came under the care of the Destitute Board. Another child, a girl of four, was sent to the Industrial School. 'Humanitarian' wrote of the 'urgent necessity' for 'the establishment of a Lying-in Hospital' since maternity cases were not admitted to the Royal Adelaide Hospital and the existing Lying-in Ward at the Asylum was over-crowded. Had a specialist maternity hospital existed, the author of the letter said, Mrs Wilson's life would probably have been saved.

Concern such as that expressed by 'Humanitarian' led to the Lying-in Home being built between 1877 and 1878. It was sited along Kintore Avenue in the quadrangle to the west of the Women's Quarters. A two-storey, bluestone and brick structure, it still exists today as part of the Migration Museum. It is a building of architectural simplicity, its only decoration the wooden cross-bars of the upper balcony. The balcony was enclosed so that 'no communication should be held from there with the street'. The home provided beds for about 30 women in three wards, an apartment for the Matron and several offices.

Ann Keenan, Jane Roberts and the other women who gave birth in the Destitute Asylum before the 1880s left the establishment after about six weeks. In September 1879 the Chairman of the Destitute Board reported that many of these women gave up their children to 'baby farmers', unregulated and often negligent foster mothers who raised the infants on bottle food. The biological mothers usually took up positions as 'wet nurses', receiving payment for suckling the babies of other, wealthier, women who wanted the advantages of having their babies breast-fed without the inconvenience of having to do it themselves.

In 1880 the Chairman of the Board made the alarming claim that less than a fifth of the children born in the Lying-in Home survived to see their first birthday. Claims such as these led to new laws which made baby farming illegal and sought to encourage bonding between mothers and babies as a means of enhancing the infant's chances of survival.

When Parliament passed the Destitute Persons Act in 1881, it was primarily concerned with the care and supervision of illegitimate children who were the responsibility of the Destitute Board, and with children nursed by foster mothers. It also made provisions for the licensing of foster mothers. According to the Act, an unmarried woman who applied for admission to the Asylum's Lying-in Home was required to sign an agreement to remain with her child at the Asylum for six months ('if her child shall so long live') and nurse it. The Board was permitted to retain care and custody of infants after this period if no satisfactory alternative was found. The Act enabled the Destitute Board to obtain declarations of paternity from unmarried mothers. It empowered the Board to license, inspect and supervise foster-mothers and wet-nurses. Under the terms of the Act foster mothers who were not licensed were liable to a fine of up to 20 pounds.

The Destitute Board continued to be concerned about the care of children under licensed foster mothers. When the Board's 'Inspectress', Mrs Kelly, drew attention to a particular foster mother they discovered that seven infants had died in her care. After a visit from the Chairman of the Board and its Medical Officer the woman's licence was cancelled. On appeal she was re-licensed to look after older children.

Social and political concern led to a Royal Commission in 1885 into the functioning of the Destitute Persons Act. According to its Final Report we know that there were 21 women and 17 infants in the Lying-in Home on the 30 June 1885 and the staff for their care consisted of a matron who was also a midwife, a cook and a general attendant. Less than 10 per cent of the total costs of the Lying-in Home were recovered from the alleged fathers of the children, but the Report noted that the laundry work done by the women off-set nearly 40 per cent of those costs.

Asylum policy divided the women admitted to the Lying-in Department into three categories: those who had only 'fallen' once and who were placed with other married women of the Asylum, those who had had children before, and those suspected of being prostitutes. The women in each category were separated from the others and restricted to their own ward and yard.

The 1885 Final Report of the Royal Commission into the Destitute Act of 1881 examined the clause which required unmarried mothers and their infants to remain in the Lying-in Department until the child was six months old. The Commission noted that the provision had been first suggested by Mr James Smith, 'one of the most experienced members of the Destitute Board', to ensure that 'the child should be nursed by its own mother until her maternal instincts are developed, and thus prevent infanticide and baby farming'. The Commissioners reported that some witnesses objected to the compulsory detention of mothers and their children while others thought it should be for a longer period. The 1885 Report mentioned that 50 of the 59 children discharged from the Lying-in Department between 1 January 1883 and September 1884 were progressing well. The Commissioners suggested that mothers be given the option of staying in the department for an additional three months.

While the Commissioners believed the Lying-in Home was 'doing a useful work in saving infant life', they did not regard its arrangements as permanent. The Report listed the three main aims of the home - 'to assist destitute women in their confinement, to secure the nursing of the child by its mother, and to preserve the mother from a further lapse into immorality'. It believed the first aim would be better served by a maternity hospital when Adelaide had reached a sufficient size to support one while it considered the other two aims 'more appropriate for a philanthropic society than for a department of the public service'.

The Commissioners expressed concern about the effect of their environment upon the women in the Lying-in Home:

> *The six months detention without a break, within the dreary wards and yards of the Lying-in Home, with no outlook beyond the high walls which surround them, and with the occupations of washing day repeated daily from Monday to Saturday every week, must be quite as irksome and more tedious and monotonous than the same term of imprisonment in a gaol. The open situation, and pleasant home-like look [of similar institutions in Melbourne] and the cheerful appearance of their inmates, present a striking contrast to the Adelaide Lying-in Home.*

ONE WOMAN'S STORY

Ada Deare was born in the Lying-in Home on 9 August 1900. She was the daughter of Lily Dear of Jamestown. When she was two or three years old Ada was fostered by a couple who made her work for them. Three days after her sixteenth birthday she married the man next door. In order to marry, Ada required the permission of a parent and she contacted Lily. They remained in touch but Lily never acknowledged publicly that Ada was her daughter. To Ada's six children she became 'Aunty Lil'. When Ada died of leukaemia at the age of 35 'Aunty Lil' kept in contact with the children.

Ada Deare as a young child

Ada with her foster parents

Ada as a young woman

Ada on her wedding day,
12 August 1916

Ada as a young matron

THE CLOSURE OF THE LYING-IN HOME

IT HAD RAINED THE NIGHT BEFORE. Adelaide Rennie had listened to the drops drumming on the roof of the Mothers' Wards as she lay in her bed there for the last time in November 1896. She had worried that the day would be wet or muggy and overcast, but the Friday morning that greeted her was bright and sunny.

Adelaide stepped out of the shadow of the verandah and looked about the courtyard of the Lying-in Home for the last time. She looked down at the child in her arms. Adelaide smoothed her son's hair before she crossed the courtyard and handed her pass out to the gatekeeper. She had no reason to look back.

Adelaide Rennie was among the increasing number of South Australian women in the paid workforce who were employed in occupations other than domestic service. After the birth of her son Adelaide returned to her job at Pearce's Boot Factory and placed the child with a licensed foster mother. Although the Factories Act of 1894 had improved Adelaide's working conditions and hours it had not increased her wages to the level of her male co-workers. This advance would not take place until after World War Two.

Adelaide was one of the 459 women who were admitted to the Lying-in Home between 1886 and 1896. Of these women 435 were unmarried. The other 24 were married, or separated, or deserted, or widows.

The Register of Admissions for 1886-1896 records that during this period there were seven stillbirths and one miscarriage at the Lying-in Home. Forty-three children died before the Destitute Board ceased monitoring their progress, when the infant was approximately two

Minnie Sax (1892-1925) was a dressmaker who gave birth to a daughter in the Lying-in Home when she was eighteen years old. Her story is tragic. The baby lived for only three months. In 1917 Minnie married a soldier who was killed in France the following year. She died of tuberculoses at the age of 33.

years old. Causes of death included debility, convulsions, diarrhoea, whooping cough and brain disease. Sadly the best intentions of the 1881 Destitute Persons Act were not enough to protect two children who died from 'want of breast milk'. One of these children was described as 'quite a skeleton' at the time of death.

The Register of Admissions gives us some of the reasons why 459 women needed the care provided by the Lying-in Home in the decade between 1886 and 1896. Although nearly half of them were able to identify the putative fathers of their children, only 46 men admitted paternity and paid maintenance. A further 25 denied proof and refused responsibility while 132 had moved away from Adelaide. A few men had died or were in gaol. Five of the women had been raped, two within their families. In 40 cases mothers were uncertain who the father of their child was. Five of these women were 'imbeciles'. The absence of proof of paternity meant that in the vast majority of cases the issue of the paternity of children born in the Lying-in Home was simply allowed to drop.

Only some of the women who gave birth in the Lying-in Home between 1886 and 1896 kept their children. Two years after the birth of their offspring over half the number of women were still with their children either with another family member, or in a refuge, or in paid work as domestic servants. However another quarter of the women gave their children over to the care of licensed foster mothers and the State Children's Council. Twenty-three children were 'adopted'. Fifty-two women married within two years of leaving the Lying-in Home, a small number in the Destitute Asylum's chapel. Twenty-six women apparently resented the continued surveillance of the Destitute Board and disappeared with their children. Four women were under the care of the Adelaide Hospital, two had died, three were in gaol and the same number were in the Lunatic Asylum at the time the Board ceased making reports on them.

Although the training of doctors in obstetric methods improved in the late nineteenth century, many of the women who passed through the Lying-in Home suffered at the hands of men who held low opinions of impoverished women. The Minutes of the Destitute Board record that on 30 January 1888 it received a letter from Dr Way of the Medical Faculty of the University of Adelaide asking if the board could 'make

Sarah Smith (1867-1951) was an eighteen year-old seamstress who gave birth to a son at the Lying-in Home in 1886. She named her employer as the child's father but had no legal proof to support her claim. She kept her son and after she married in 1896 had another four children.

arrangements for the attendance on the Midwifery Destitute cases to be carried out in future by the University Medical Authorities to enable the students of the Medical School to acquire a practical knowledge of midwifery'. On 9 April the Minutes recorded that two medical students had been referred to the Board and would 'be sent for at the next cases occurring on the Asylum site'. In 1895 a member of Parliament stated that these students held the destitute pregnant women of the Lying-in Home in such contempt that 'they would come to the Asylum for amusement and to laugh, and poke fun at the women in their pain'.

Audrey Lady Tennyson, wife of Governor Tennyson, visited the Destitute Asylum's Lying-in Home numerous times around the turn of the century. In a letter dated 24 May 1899 she described her first visit to the 'workhouse' in which she and a companion 'went to a separate building with a separate garden where no-one is ever allowed except the clergy, doctor, or relations, so that no one may know the girls have been there. This is only for the first time of falling. I was horrified to find 19 there either with their babies or waiting for them, one a girl of 14'. In language with reflects contemporary attitudes to lying-in women Lady Tennyson noted that if women 'offended a second time they go to the general lying-in ward'. In 1900 she recorded that a 'charming matron' told her most of the first 'offenders' were 'nice quiet well-behaved' young women. The Matron no doubt shocked the genteel Governor's wife when she told her of a 'poor thing' who was a

> *case of The Cenci [incest], ... the girl was only sixteen and a half and they came to fetch her away to the Reformatory for eighteen months, and the poor girl clung to and fought for her baby and begged and entreated not to be separated from it. It was too heartrending for words and at last, instead of boarding it out with strangers - her own mother was allowed to take it, which somewhat consoled her.*

Lady Tennyson, like many other prominent women, was involved in the public sphere of South Australian life. She played a significant part in the opening of the Queen Victoria Maternity Home in 1902. This establishment, the introduction of the Commonwealth Maternity Bonus of 1912 and the extension of the Queen Victoria's facilities to unmarried women in 1917 all contributed to the decline of the Lying-in Home during the early years of the twentieth century. It closed its doors for the last time in 1918.

Olive Doran was born in the Lying-in Home in 1885. Her unmarried mother died when Olive was eight years old and she was sent to live with her father's parents who never acknowledged her as their granddaughter. Olive later had nine children of her own. This photograph was taken when she was in her 50s.

APPENDIX 1

Number of destitute poor in the Asylum

YEAR	WOMEN	MEN	CHILDREN
1869	55	119	190
1878	102	188	155
1888	126	238	3
1898	116	243	2
1908	141	267	3

Source: South Australia, Parliament, *Papers*

The Migration Museum wishes to thank the following descendants of some of the women who lived 'behind the wall' for their help: Mrs Brenda Baker, Mrs G. H. Carnell, Mrs Glory Dudley, Mrs Lilian Holberton, Mr Laurie Pearson, Mr Larnor Ritchie and Mr Tony Schar.

Opposite: *This photograph of May Mahoney, who was born in the Destitute Asylum in the 1890s, is much loved by visitors to the Migration Museum in the 1990s. Courtesy Mrs P. Alford*

Key years in the social history of women in

South Australia

1836   The first Europeans settle in South Australia. Among other
        duties the Emigration Agent provides work at reduced
        wages for male immigrants when the labour market is over-
        supplied and distributes rations to new settlers who are poor
        or sick when they disembark, or who are proven to be alone
        and unable to support themselves.

1840   The South Australian Colonization Commissioners in
        London tell the Colonial Office and the Treasury that they
        have no money.

1841   Economic crisis in the colony.

1843   The government of South Australia passes its first
        legislation to deal with poverty, the 'Act to provide for the
        maintenance and relief of deserted Wives and Children and
        other destitute persons'. The Act states that three
        generations of relatives are responsible for supporting
        family members who are unable to work.

1849   The Emigration Agent relocates from Adelaide to its port.
        As a result the Colonial Secretary writes to leading
        members of the Church of England, Roman Catholic,
        Presbyterian and Congregationalist branches of Christianity
        in the colony to invite them to join a Destitute Board to
        provide support to the needy from the huts in Emigration

Square. In December 1849 the Board provides relief to 25 indoor and 114 outdoor destitute persons.

1851   In this year accommodation at the 'Destitute Asylum' in the West Parklands becomes inadequate. In December 1851 the Board provides relief to 63 indoor, and 187 outdoor cases of poverty.

1852   The Destitute Board is granted temporary use of the Police Barracks on North Terrace. The Adelaide Female Immigration Depot is established.

1856   In March a Select Committee of the Legislative Council of South Australian Parliament reports on Excessive Female Immigration and Destitution in the colony.

1856   In June the South Australian Constitution Act establishes responsible government in the colony. Adult males require a property qualification to vote for the Legislative Council. Electors for the House of Assembly have to have lived in the colony for six months. Women are not granted the vote for either House of Parliament.

1856   Women are prominent in the Female Refuge founded in this year.

1856   Adelaide Female Immigration Depot is closed.

1857   Women first use petitions to voice their political opinion: they present 73 signatures to Parliament against legislation enabling a man to marry his sister-in-law after the death of his wife.

1858   A Matrimonial Causes Act is passed in South Australian Parliament. Although this Act facilitates divorce and judicial separation it is weighted heavily in favour of the husband. While adultery is deemed sufficient grounds for a husband to divorce his wife, this is not seen as adequate grounds for a wife to divorce her husband. Women requesting divorce have to cite additional 'degrading circumstances' such as bigamy or incest. However, this Act does protect the property rights of deserted wives.

1861   South Australia becomes the first colony in Australia to entitle women to vote in local council elections through the Municipal Corporation Act.

1863   An 'Act for the regulation of the Asylum for the Destitute Poor' empowers the Governor to make rules for the management of the Asylum and imposes penalties upon inmates who break these rules.

1866-67   The Destitute Person's Relief Act formally establishes the Destitute Board.

1876   A greater proportion of women to men in the State's population means that some women can never marry. Economic depression makes the idea of middle-class women in the workforce more acceptable than before. Education for women becomes more important. The University of Adelaide accepts women in its first classes. The Adelaide Children's Hospital - the result of work by a committee of eight women - opens its doors.

1877   Catherine Helen Spence becomes the first woman to serve on a public Board. She joins the Advanced School for Girls' Board of Advice.

1879   The Advanced School for Girls opens.

1880   The British government agrees to South Australian legislation permitting women to undertake degrees. The Adelaide Creche, founded and run by women, opens.

During the 1880s and 1890s there is a significant increase in the size of the paid female workforce in South Australia. The participation of all women aged between 15 and 60 rises from 24.9 per cent in 1871 to 32.9 per cent in 1891. At this time there is a steady decline in the proportion of women engaged in domestic service and an increase of their numbers in manufacturing and commerce.

1881   The Destitute Person's Act aims to eliminate the evils of 'baby farming'.

1882   The Social Purity Society is founded. It succeeds in making Parliament change the age of consent from 12 to 16 years in an effort to halt child prostitution. It plays an important part in the evolution of the female suffrage movement.

1883   South Australian Parliament passes the Married Women's Property Act which allows married women to own property in their own name.

1883-84 The Custody of Infants Act introduces limited reforms which in some instances enables mothers to gain custody of their children.

1885   In July Dr E.C. Stirling, Member for North Adelaide, proposes an extension of the franchise, for the Legislative Council, to unmarried women who meet the property qualification imposed upon male electors.

1885   In October the Second and Final Report of the Royal Commission appointed to Report on the Destitute Person's Act of 1881 is tabled in Parliament.

1886   The Destitute Person's Act Amendment Act establishes the State Children's Council. Catherine Helen Spence becomes a member of the Council.

1887   The Guardianship of Infants Act gives women equal rights of guardianship of children upon the dissolution of a marriage.

1888   The Female Suffrage League is formed and joins forces with the Women's Christian Temperance Union (founded 1886).

1890   The Working Women's Trades Union is formed in response
        to the abuse of employing cheap female and child labour
        known as 'sweating'. This organisation is to play an
        important part in securing the franchise for women.

1892   A Factories and Shops Commission to investigate 'sweating'
        is established partly as a result of agitation by the
        W.W.T.U. leaders.

1894   South Australian women win the right to vote. The
        Factories Act establishes regulations for the inspection of
        factories.

1895   Mrs Augusta Zadow is appointed as the first female
        Inspector of Factories. Also in this year Catherine Helen
        Spence becomes the first woman in Australia to participate
        in an official commission. She is appointed to the
        Commission of Enquiry into the Adelaide Hospital.

1895   State Children's Act transfers regulation of licensed foster
        mothers from the Destitute Board to State Children's
        Council.

1896   The Married Women's Protection Act secures maintenance
        for wives forced to leave their husbands due to 'physical or
        moral cruelty'.

1901   The Australian colonies federate as the Commonwealth of
        Australia.

1902   Australian women are granted the right to vote in
        Commonwealth elections and to stand for Federal
        Parliament.

1902   The Queen Victoria Maternity Home is opened.

1907   The Harvester Judgement in the Federal Court establishes
        the family wage as opposed to equal pay for women and
        men. Women are paid 54 per cent of the male wage
        because it is assumed that men have to support a family.

1909	The Federal government introduces an Aged Pension.
1910	An 'Act for the Relief of Persons whose Relatives liable to support them reside in another State of the Commonwealth and for other purposes' is passed in Federal Parliament.
1911	The South Australian government introduces a widows' pension and empowers the Destitute Board to make cash payments to ill or injured persons.
1912	The Commonwealth government introduces a maternity allowance.
1914	World War I begins. The first female Justices of the Peace and police officers are appointed.
1917	The Old Folks Home openes at Magill and the Destitute Asylum is closed.
1917	The Queen Victoria Maternity Home extends its facilities to unmarried mothers.
1918	The Lying-in Home is closed.

LIST OF SOURCES

Primary Sources

DESTITUTE ASYLUM RECORDS

Government Record Group 28/1
Minutes of the Destitute Board 1849-56, 1870-1927

Government Record Group 28/5
Register of Admissions to the Destitute Asylum 1870-73, 1881-1924

Government Record Group 28/13
Register of Admissions to the Lying-in Home 1886-96

SOUTH AUSTRALIAN PARLIAMENT

South Australia, *Statutes*:
An Act to provide for the maintenance and relief of deserted wives and children ..., 6 Victoria No. 11 1843

An Act for the regulation of the Asylum for the Destitute Poor and other purposes. No. 2 1863

Destitute Persons Relief Act No. 12 1866-67

Destitute Persons Relief and Industrial Reformatory Schools Act No. 26 1872

The Destitute Persons Act Amendment Act No. 387
1886

SOUTH AUSTRALIA, PARLIAMENT, *PAPERS*

Reports of the Select Committee of the Legislative
Council of South Australia appointed to inquire into the
Excessive Female Immigration 2 No. 137   1856

Destitute Board Regulations No. 27   1867

First Progress Report of Commission appointed to
Report on the Destitute Act 1881, 4 No. 228 1883-84

Second and Final Report of Commission appointed to
Report on the Destitute Act 1881, 4 No. 228   1885

LIST OF SOURCES

Secondary Sources

BOOKS

Daniels, K. and Murnane, M.
Australia's Women: A Documentary History, University
of Queensland Press, Queensland, 1989.

Dickey, B.
*Rations, Residence, Resources: A History of Social
Welfare in South Australia since 1836*, Wakefield Press,
Adelaide, 1986.

Hasluck, Alexandra (Ed.)
*Audrey Tennyson's Vice-Regal Days The Australian
letters of Audrey Lady Tennyson 1899-1903*, National
Library of Australia, Canberra, 1978.

Jones, H.
In Her Own Name: Women in South Australian History,
Wakefield Press, Adelaide, 1986.

Parham, D.
Architecture of the Destitute Asylum Adelaide, Flinders
University Art Museum, 1983.

Public Buildings Department
*South Australian Museum Redevelopment Heritage
Study*, Public Buildings Department, 1988.
THESES

De Vries, G.D.,
'Conditions of Childbirth in Adelaide', B.A. (Hons)
Thesis, University of Adelaide, 1963.

ARTICLES

Bacci, C.
'The "Woman Question" ', chapter 15 in *The Flinders
History of South Australia: Social History*
(ed.) E. Richards, Wakefield Press, Adelaide, 1986.

Dare, R.
'Paupers' Rights: Governor Grey and the Poor Law in
South Australia', *Australian Historical Studies*, vol. 25,
No. 99, October 1992, pp 220-243.

Nance, C.
'The Destitute in Early Colonial South Australia',
Journal of the Historical Society of South Australia,
vol 7, 1980, pp 46-61.

Nicol, R.
"A Slanderous Parson and a Soaped Over Pauper
Woman": The Ultimate Fate of the Destitute in Colonial
South Australia'. *Journal of the Historical Society of
South Australia*, vol 17, 1989, pp 39-61.

Sumerling, P.
'The Darker Side of Motherhood: Abortion and
Infanticide in South Australia 1870-1910', *Journal of the
Historical Society of South Australia*, vol 13, 1985,
pp 111-127.